MW00423787

FRIENDSHIP

PUBLISHED BY LIFEWAY PRESS®

NASHVILLE, TENNESSEE

AUTHORS:
Kenny Luck
Todd Wendorff
Stephen Arterburn

TEAM LEADER, PUBLISHING:
Brian Daniel

ART DIRECTOR & DESIGNERS:
Christi Kearney
Heather Wetherington

PRODUCTION DESIGNER:
Denise Wells

CONTENT EDITOR:
Gena Rogers

PRODUCTION EDITOR:
Juliana Duncan

VIDEO DIRECTOR:
Frank Baker

VIDEO EDITOR:
Phil LeBeau

DIRECTOR, ADULT MINISTRY PUBLISHING
Philip Nation

Friendship: Transform Through Strong Relationships Workbook

Published by LifeWay Press®
Reprinted 2015

kennyluck.com; everymanministries.com;
facebook.com/KennyLuck; twitter.com/kenny_luck

©2013 Kenny Luck and Todd Wendorff

Published by arrangement with The WaterBrook Multnomah Publishing Group, a division of Random House, Inc.

ISBN: 978-1-4158-7335-9

Item: 005493292

Dewey Decimal Classification: 248.842

Subject Headings: MEN \ FRIENDSHIP \ CHRISTIAN LIFE

Unless otherwise noted, Scripture quotations are taken from the Holman Christian Standard Bible®, Copyright 1999, 2000, 2002, 2003 by Holman Bible Publishers. Used by permission. Scriptures marked NIV are from the Holy Bible, New International Version, copyright © 1973, 1978, 1984 by International Bible Society. Scripture quotations marked (NLT) are taken from the Holy Bible, New Living Translation, copyright © 1996. Used by permission of Tyndale House Publishers, Inc., Wheaton, IL 60189 USA. All rights reserved.

To order additional copies of this resource, order online at www.lifeway.com; write LifeWay Men: One LifeWay Plaza, Nashville, TN 37234-0152; fax order to (615) 251-5933; call toll-free (800) 458-2772.

Printed in the United States of America

Adult Ministry Publishing
LifeWay Church Resources
One LifeWay Plaza
Nashville, TN 37234-0152

Contents

How to Use This Study Guide

Welcome to an eight-week journey into understanding the importance of godly friendships and how God designs them to complete us spiritually. Before you get started, here is some helpful information about the different elements you'll encounter within the study:

KEY VERSES AND GOALS FOR GROWTH // Review these items as you prepare for each group meeting. They reveal the focus of the study for the week, will be referenced in Kenny's video message, and will be used in the Connect with the Word personal study time.

INTRODUCTION // This is designed to introduce your study for the week. You will want to read this before your group meets so you'll better understand the topic and the context for your time together.

PERSONAL TIME: CONNECT WITH THE WORD // Complete the Connect with the Word section before each small-group meeting. Consider this section your personal Bible study for the week.

GROUP TIME: REVIEW // The first question in this section is designed to provide you with an opportunity to talk about what God has been revealing to you in your personal time with Him during the past week. The second question is an icebreaker to help you ease into the study topic.

GROUP TIME: VIDEO TEACHING // This listening guide gives you an opportunity to fill in the blanks on important points as you view the video message from Kenny.

GROUP TIME: VIDEO FEEDBACK // This section is designed to facilitate follow-up discussion regarding what you heard from the video message and how you were affected.

GROUP TIME: CONNECT WITH THE GROUP // This portion of your weekly meeting will give you an opportunity to connect with the other men in your group by discussing truths from the Scriptures and the topic for the week and encouraging one another.

WRAP // This section serves as a conclusion to the group time and summarizes key points from your group meeting each week.

Spiritual Castaways

Remember the movie *Cast Away*? Chuck Noland is riding in a FedEx cargo plane when it drifts off course somewhere over the Pacific Ocean and loses communications in the middle of a typhoon. Before the crew can reestablish radio contact, the plane crashes into the ocean. Miraculously, Chuck survives and washes ashore. And so begins his long and painful odyssey as a castaway.

Fast-forward to his miraculous rescue four years later. ... Chuck's old girlfriend reminisces with him about the rescue efforts at the time of his disappearance. She spreads out the old search grid and shows Chuck where the effort had focused, based on the original flight plan. Then she slides her finger hundreds of miles across the map to where he was actually rescued. The inability of the pilot to report his position, combined with a slow drift off course, sealed Chuck's fate and doomed the rescue before it began.

We're only talking about a Hollywood movie, but just as severed communication doomed Chuck to being a lonely castaway, the lack of communication and connection among men has created a whole culture of spiritual castaways. Pulled off course in their walks with God, not reporting their personal or spiritual status to anyone, men become isolated. No one really knows them or where they are in their private struggles. Time passes, and when the typhoons of temptation strike, they drift off course. Unfortunately, many men don't even have the chance to get rescued because they were never checking in with anyone.

We are traveling through life unconnected and unexamined, carefully projecting an image that says, "I'm OK," but privately battling inner turmoil and conflict that stem from life's normal pressures.

We need to connect. We were designed to connect.

As you proceed through this Bible study, determine to hold up a mirror to your life and ask yourself some tough questions. Spend time in personal reflection and honest dialogue with God and other men. Whether you are doing this study individually or in a group, realize that honesty with yourself, with God, and with others will produce the greatest results.

Our prayer is that you will be moved to embrace God's plan for friendship and will experience His promised blessings as you risk going deeper in your relationships with other men.

The Myth of Isolation

The number-one dilemma facing God's men today is isolation. More than any other time in history, men feel emotionally and relationally cut off from other men. If it weren't so, they wouldn't be spending billions of dollars on sexually explicit Internet sites to find relief from their loneliness. Sure, we have friends and we lead busy lives, but as a general condition, males are not connected to one another for any deep purposes.

goals for growth

☐ Understand the danger of isolation

☐ Recognize that isolation stunts spiritual growth and opens us up to spiritual attack

☐ Commit to ending relational or emotional isolation

When a guy is under pressure or his relationships are suffering or life has simply thrown him one too many curves, he tends to keep his suffering to himself. This isn't healthy for any man, and it's a definite no-no for God's man. You see, there's more to isolation than just not having someone to talk to. Isolation weakens our defenses. We are engaged in a spiritual battle every day, and one side or the other is winning at each moment. So the question is, *Who will prevail in the various domains of your life today—the dark forces aligned with the world and the Devil, or God and His kingdom?*

Overcoming isolation is not about getting and giving warm fuzzies or an occasional high-five. It involves a war for your spiritual well-being, your effectiveness for God, and your impact on those closest to you. What God's man needs to clearly understand is that isolation from other men is not just bad, it's deadly.

KEY VERSES

---

[9] *Two are better than one because they have a good reward for their efforts.* [10] *For if either falls, his companion can lift him up; but pity the one who falls without another to lift him up.* [11] *Also, if two lie down together, they can keep warm; but how can one person alone keep warm?* [12] *And if someone overpowers one person, two can resist him. A cord of three strands is not easily broken.* (Ecclesiastes 4:9-12)

Be serious! Be alert! Your adversary the Devil is prowling around like a roaring lion, looking for anyone he can devour. (1 Peter 5:8)

NOTES

CONNECT WITH THE WORD

THIS SECTION IS DESIGNED TO BE A PERSONAL BIBLE STUDY
EXPERIENCE FOR YOU TO COMPLETE BEFORE YOUR SMALL-GROUP
SESSION EACH WEEK. COME TO YOUR GROUP MEETING PREPARED
TO SHARE YOUR RESPONSES AND PERSONAL APPLICATIONS. YOU
MAY WANT TO MARK OR HIGHLIGHT ANY QUESTIONS THAT WERE
PARTICULARLY MEANINGFUL TO YOU. BEFORE YOU BEGIN YOUR
STUDY, READ THE SCRIPTURES ON PAGE 8.

1. Read Ecclesiastes 4:9-12. What are the downsides of isolation?
What are the upsides of supportive friendships?

2. When is the condition of isolation most clearly seen and felt?

3. When an isolated man falls down, what happens?

4. Why do you think Solomon used the word "pity" to describe an isolated man who has fallen? What obvious outcomes elicit sorrow for that man?

5. Read 1 Peter 5:8. Why is Satan compared to a lion? What does this imply about his approach or methods of attack?

6. What is the Devil's constant preoccupation?

7. What factors give a lion the best chance for catching and killing its prey? What factors make it more difficult?

REVIEW

What are your expectations of this study?

What do you see as the dangers of living your life like a spiritual castaway? What do you see as the benefits of living life in community with other men?

VIDEO TEACHING

BELOW YOU WILL FIND A LISTENING GUIDE THAT GIVES YOU AN OPPORTUNITY TO FOLLOW IMPORTANT POINTS AS YOU VIEW THE MESSAGE FROM KENNY. WE'LL UNPACK THIS INFORMATION TOGETHER AFTER THE VIDEO.

Watch Video Session 1: "The Myth of Isolation" (11:57).

The single greatest attack that men have to fear is isolation—

being _____, _____, and

_____ cut off from other men.

God's man is never instructed to self-diagnose his

own _____.

You need friends, not _____.

IF YOU MISSED THIS WEEK'S VIDEO VISIT LIFEWAY.COM/FRIENDSHIP TO GET CAUGHT UP.

VIDEO FEEDBACK

 In his video message, Kenny asks a number of questions related to our friendships with men in our lives:

- Are your friendships stretching you to greatness where it really counts?
- Are your friendships sharpening you spiritually?
- Does your wife or the woman in your life see your friendships as critical to her own well-being?
- Do your friendships keep you out of the muddy waters of moral compromise?
- Does your inner circle always tell you what you want to hear or is it healthy enough to sometimes tell you what you need to hear?
- Do your friendships get you the wins where you need them the most?
- Do your friends see who you really are?

Based on how you answered these questions, how would you rate yourself in the area of pursuing friendships with other men? Explain your response to the group.

1	10
I pretty much go it on my own.	I'm connected to a support system of men, and we do life together.

What concrete actions can you take this week to move closer to the right side of this scale?

CONNECT WITH THE GROUP

When my wife Chrissy asked me to rally the men of our couples group to help move a family, I (Kenny) reluctantly agreed (because I *hate* to help move). Who enjoys lugging heavy refrigerators and tons of boxes, especially when it's somebody else's junk? But Chrissy had become acquainted with Tina (the wife) at church, and she saw an opportunity for us to meet a need. Tina's husband Hans was certainly grateful when so many helping hands showed up that Saturday morning.

The next time I ran into Hans was a month later at church. I asked him how the move finished up and then admitted that I thought God used the move to bring us together that day. When I said that, his eyes immediately filled with tears.

"Hans, are you OK?"

"I was so alone," he choked out.

"What did you say?" I didn't think I had heard him correctly.

He took a deep breath and said again, very clearly, "Kenny, I was so alone."

In that moment, Hans defined what I believe is the number-one dilemma facing Christian men: isolation.[1]

1. **What is the primary way you cope during times of isolation and loneliness?**

2. **Do you have friends in your life right now who know about your true state of life? About your times of loneliness? About the times you fall down or sin? What can you do to deepen these friendships? If you don't have friends like this, what steps can you take to begin developing close friendships with other men?**

3. When, if ever, has your isolation negatively impacted your spiritual life? Your relationships? Your marriage?

4. In what area(s) of your life are you being overpowered by the roaring lion (1 Peter 5:8)? Have you opened up to another man about it? If not, why?

We helped Hans and Tina move everything that day, including their redwood Jacuzzi. While moving is not my first choice for male bonding, there's something about carrying furniture and lifting boxes that bonds people. By the end of the day I felt we were beginning a special friendship.

5. Why do you think men continue living isolated and defeated spiritual lives? What lies do you think Satan tells a man to keep him isolated and open to attack?

6. What can we do as a group to protect one another from becoming isolated?

7. Write a one-sentence prayer expressing to God your desire to overcome isolation and connect more deeply with other men.

1. Adapted from Stephen Arterburn and Kenny Luck, *Every Man, God's Man* (Colorado Springs: WaterBrook Press, 2003), 141.

WRAP

Men do not become men in the company of women. We become men in the company of other men. This is the way God wants His men to go. Wherever you find men watching one another's backs and caring enough to confront in order to help a friend become God's man, you find men who are growing their characters and spiritual lives, men who no longer live as spiritual castaways.

Remember these key thoughts from this week's study:
- The number-one dilemma facing God's men today is isolation.
- When a guy is under pressure, he tends to keep his suffering to himself.
- Pursuing healthy friendship is a way of life that provides help when we need it most.
- Isolation from other men is not just bad, it's deadly.

PRAY TOGETHER

The Command to Connect

The apostle Paul wrote to Corinthian men, "The eye can never say to the hand, 'I don't need you.' The head can't say to the feet, 'I don't need you.'" (1 Corinthians 12:21, NLT). His point was clear: Stop acting as if you don't need one another. What he knew, and what we see, is that when men are doing life with other men who share their commitment to spiritual growth, they can sustain their momentum and achieve personal changes faster than if they attempt to go it alone. No big mystery; that's God's plan.

goals for growth

☐ Realize that connecting with other men is not optional

☐ Understand that connecting with other men is of practical importance to your spiritual growth

☐ Commit to pursuing and deepening male friendships

We need to connect with men in significant communication regarding every domain of life, dealing candidly with the specific dynamics unique to men in marriage, career, and parenting.

Men become men in the company of other men. For God's man, who wants to do life God's way, connecting with other men is not optional.

KEY VERSES

[20] Now in a large house there are not only gold and silver bowls, but also those of wood and clay, some for honorable use, some for dishonorable. [21] So if anyone purifies himself from anything dishonorable, he will be a special instrument, set apart, useful to the Master, prepared for every good work.

[22] Flee from youthful passions, and pursue righteousness, faith, love, and peace, along with those who call on the Lord from a pure heart.

(2 Timothy 2:20-22)

[13] Encourage each other daily, while it is still called today, so that none of you is hardened by sin's deception. ...

[23] Let us hold on to the confession of our hope without wavering, for He who promised is faithful. [24] And let us be concerned about one another in order to promote love and good works, [25] not staying away from our worship meetings, as some habitually do, but encouraging each other, and all the more as you see the day drawing near.

(Hebrews 3:13; 10:23-25)

NOTES

CONNECT WITH THE WORD

THIS SECTION IS DESIGNED TO BE A PERSONAL BIBLE STUDY
EXPERIENCE FOR YOU TO COMPLETE BEFORE YOUR SMALL-GROUP
SESSION EACH WEEK. COME TO YOUR GROUP MEETING PREPARED
TO SHARE YOUR RESPONSES AND PERSONAL APPLICATIONS. YOU
MAY WANT TO MARK OR HIGHLIGHT ANY QUESTIONS THAT WERE
PARTICULARLY MEANINGFUL TO YOU. BEFORE YOU BEGIN YOUR
STUDY, READ THE SCRIPTURES ON PAGE 20.

1. Read 2 Timothy 2:20-22. What's the central message of verse 20?

2. According to verse 22, what will play a critical role for God's
man in reaching his spiritual goals? Why do you think Timothy's
friend and mentor, Paul, stressed this?

3. In practical terms, what do you think it means to "pursue
righteousness" with other men?

4. What does this passage imply about how we should fight temptation?

5. Read Hebrews 3:13 and 10:23-25. What specific encouragements are mentioned in these verses? How are they connected?

6. What are the goals of friendship according to these verses?

7. What are God's men mindful of as they encourage and sharpen one another in their faith (v. 25)? Why is that important?

REVIEW

What has the Lord revealed to you over the past week regarding coming out of isolation?

What is your primary purpose in friendship? Does it line up with the purpose described in Hebrews 3:13 and 10:24? Explain.

VIDEO TEACHING

▶ BELOW YOU WILL FIND A LISTENING GUIDE THAT GIVES YOU AN OPPORTUNITY TO FOLLOW IMPORTANT POINTS AS YOU VIEW THE MESSAGE FROM KENNY. WE'LL UNPACK THIS INFORMATION TOGETHER AFTER THE VIDEO.

Watch Video Session 2: "The Command to Connect" (11:39).

God says that connecting with other men for the purpose of spiritual growth and accountability is not an _Option_ .

Run _Away_ from temptation.
Run _Towards_ God's purposes.
Run _With_ a group of men who are running after God's purposes.

When you're _Disconnected_ not only do you suffer, but your other relationships suffer.

When you _Connect_ and become more healthy, the other relationships in your life become more healthy.

IF YOU MISSED THIS WEEK'S VIDEO VISIT
LIFEWAY.COM/FRIENDSHIP **TO GET CAUGHT UP.**

VIDEO FEEDBACK

1. Run *away* from temptation.
2. Run *toward* God's purposes.
3. Run *with* a group of men who are running after God's purposes.

Which of these steps do you find easiest? Most difficult? Explain your response to the group.

Kenny talks about God's choice for you—consistent connection with God's men. What is your understanding of why He wants this for you so badly that He commands it?

CONNECT WITH THE GROUP

When we ask guys if they are connected spiritually somewhere, they often reply that they are in a couples' Bible study. Then we ask them if, in their couples' group, they talk about their struggles with porn on the Internet or with attractive women in the office.

The fact is, when we're in the company of women—including our wives—we simply don't discuss the things we need to deal with as men. And lust and temptation aren't the only topics we need to talk about.

1. What is your level of connection with other men right now? What specific struggles or frustrations have you experienced when you've tried to connect on a deeper level?

2. When, if ever, have you connected with another man on a deeper level? What do you think helped you connect this way?

3. In 2 Timothy 2:22, Paul encouraged Timothy to connect with other godly men. In light of this passage, consider your three closest friendships and, on a scale of 1 to 10 (1=poor; 10=excellent), rate your level of connection in the areas of encouragement, honesty, and integrity.

Friend: _____
Encouragement: _____ Honesty: _____ Integrity: _____

Friend: _____
Encouragement: _____ Honesty: _____ Integrity: _____

Friend: _____
Encouragement: _____ Honesty: _____ Integrity: _____

Share your ratings with the group and then discuss what specific actions you can take to develop close friendships or deepen your connection in existing ones.

4. To what extent do you think you are spiritually connected with other men? Explain.

Some of us who feel unconnected choose avenues of relief and comfort outside of God's plan which bring harm to our relationship with Him and with others. At every men's conference we lead, we encounter men who fess up to using Internet porn, having illicit affairs, and ingesting substances their bodies were not designed to handle. Others immerse themselves in their work, a sports team, or some hobby to deal with the stresses of life. Unfortunately, these diversions are exactly that—diversions. They don't make us better men. We have found that men who are not progressing personally, spiritually, or relationally are in those ruts because they will not risk connecting with another man.

5. What risks are you willing to take to achieve a connection with other men that produces significant spiritual gains?

6. Write down a specific request you would like to see God answer regarding your friendships:

WRAP

Connecting with other men is not optional. It's how God intended us to live. We need to be real with one another about our progress in commitment to Jesus Christ as He seeks to influence our marriages, careers, and parenting.

Remember these key thoughts from this week's study:
- Connecting with other men is of practical importance to your spiritual growth.
- Men become men in the company of other men.
- You will feel unconnected when you choose avenues of relief and comfort outside of God's plan.
- God's choice for you is consistent connection with God's men.

PRAY TOGETHER

Connecting
to Character

We all remember the cliques in junior high and high school. Kids usually fell into one of several categories: jocks, nerds, the in-crowd, band geeks, stoners, or honor students. Each clique had its own lingo, ways of thinking, and lists of activities or qualifications to officially belong. Which clique did you identify with? The myth is that we will eventually grow out of the clique mentality, become more tolerant of different kinds of people, and become independent and mature. The reality is that cliques and their influence among men survive and thrive. As adults, we simply call cliques "our friends," but many of the dynamics are identical. We still gravitate toward people who act like us, look like us, like the things we like, and do what we do—for better or for worse. The one big difference between then and now is that much more is at stake, especially for God's man.

Like meat soaking in a marinade, we soak up the character of our close friends. As Proverbs 13:20 says, "The one who walks with the wise will become wise, but a companion of fools will suffer harm." Our friends rub off on us, both consciously and subconsciously, which leads to changes in our convictions and conduct. So the question is: *Who is rubbing off on you?*

goals for growth

☐ Realize the importance of character in choosing our friends

☐ Recognize the impact that others' character has on us

☐ Commit to developing both godly character and godly relationships

KEY VERSES

The one who walks with the wise will become wise,
but a companion of fools will suffer harm. *(Proverbs 13:20)*

¹ I will sing of faithful love and justice;
I will sing praise to You, LORD.
² I will pay attention to the way of integrity.
When will You come to me?
I will live with a heart of integrity in my house.
³ I will not set anything worthless before my eyes.
I hate the practice of transgression;
it will not cling to me.
⁴ A devious heart will be far from me;
I will not be involved with evil.
⁵ I will destroy anyone
who secretly slanders his neighbor;
I cannot tolerate anyone
with haughty eyes or an arrogant heart.
⁶ My eyes favor the faithful of the land
so that they may sit down with me.
The one who follows the way of integrity
may serve me.
⁷ No one who acts deceitfully
will live in my palace;
no one who tells lies
will remain in my presence.
⁸ Every morning I will destroy
all the wicked of the land,
eliminating all evildoers from the LORD's city. *(Psalm 101)*

NOTES

CONNECT WITH THE WORD

THIS SECTION IS DESIGNED TO BE A PERSONAL BIBLE STUDY
EXPERIENCE FOR YOU TO COMPLETE BEFORE YOUR SMALL-GROUP
SESSION EACH WEEK. COME TO YOUR GROUP MEETING PREPARED
TO SHARE YOUR RESPONSES AND PERSONAL APPLICATIONS. YOU
MAY WANT TO MARK OR HIGHLIGHT ANY QUESTIONS THAT WERE
PARTICULARLY MEANINGFUL TO YOU. BEFORE YOU BEGIN YOUR
STUDY, READ THE SCRIPTURES ON PAGE 32.

1. Read Psalm 101. What are the specific character qualities David
wanted for his life?

2. What character quality was he looking for in his associates?
Why? What did David believe was literally at stake?

3. What warning signs tipped him off to the types of men he
didn't want to hang with (vv. 4-7)?

4. What role did faithful men play in David's life (v. 6)?

5. At the end of the psalm, what was David's conclusion about who he would allow to influence him?

6. Which character quality described in Psalm 101 inspires you most? Why?

REVIEW

What has the Lord revealed to you over the past week regarding making consistent connection with God's men a part of your life?

Which clique did you identify with when you were in school? Did that group of people influence the person you are today? How so?

VIDEO TEACHING

BELOW YOU WILL FIND A LISTENING GUIDE THAT GIVES YOU AN OPPORTUNITY TO FOLLOW IMPORTANT POINTS AS YOU VIEW THE MESSAGE FROM KENNY. WE'LL UNPACK THIS INFORMATION TOGETHER AFTER THE VIDEO.

Watch Video Session 3: "Connecting to Character" (09:00).

Godly character is synonymous with _____

_____ with godly men.

God's man must _____ _____ other godly men.

Through the ages, God's men who have respected God's Word have sought God's men so that they could _____

_____ _____ in their lives.

IF YOU MISSED THIS WEEK'S VIDEO VISIT LIFEWAY.COM/FRIENDSHIP TO GET CAUGHT UP.

VIDEO FEEDBACK

 In his video message, Kenny really drills down on Psalm 101:6:

My eyes will be on the faithful in the land,
that they may dwell with me;
the one whose walk is blameless
will minister to me. (NIV)

Consider the following questions and talk about your responses with the group:

What type of people do you choose to associate with?

Are they the "faithful in the land"?

Do you have faithful people in your life?

Who do you choose to "dwell" with?

Who ministers to you?

CONNECT WITH THE GROUP

Junior high was rough for me (Todd). I decided to rebel against authority and see what it was like. I had a very strong father who was "The Law" in our home. I had just completed five years of private school and was sick of following the rules. So I began to experiment with drugs and alcohol. My friends didn't help much. They had uninvolved parents and ultimate freedom to do anything they wanted. We'd wander the hill I grew up on and look for ways to be juvenile delinquents.

The final straw came when my father went to school and discovered the incredibly disrespectful attitude I'd developed toward my teachers. The next evening he called me into his den— an intimidating room where his safari animal trophies stared at me from the walls. He had a three-decker organ in one corner of the room, and a couch, coffee table, and desk in the other. The minute I walked in, I knew I was toast.

1. What were your middle school and high school years like? In what ways can you relate to Todd's experience?

2. Which childhood friends were good for you? Which were bad influences? Why?

That evening when my dad called me into his den, all he had to say was, "Son, I've been to school, and I know what's going on." I fell into his arms and began to weep. As I wept, he told me one thing I will never forget: "Todd, there are two roads in life, and you are headed down the wrong one." He then told me to go to school the next day and change my friends. Cut it off at the root; eliminate the influence to change the behavior.

3. How would you describe your closest friends today? How do their priorities line up with your own?

4. How do you know when a friend is influencing you negatively?

My dad's advice worked. The next day I abandoned my old friends and searched out a new crowd. My new friends were athletes and were heavily involved in school. Everything changed for me that year.

5. What specific indicators tell you that you need to break away from a friend or friends and find new ones? What steps do you need to take to make that break?

6. What character qualities make you a positive influence on your friends? What about you is rubbing off on them?

Pray for your friends, asking God to empower you to help them become all that He made them to be. Also pray for an opportunity to be used this week in the life of a friend. Or, if you have let an opportunity slip through the cracks, commit now to help in a practical way.

WRAP

Maybe Garth Brooks was right. When you have friends in low places, you'll have plenty of company to help you drown your blues away. But what if your friends are contributing to your problems? Research shows that who you are is a function of who you know. Your friends help shape your outlook, values, emotions, and behaviors. Their influence can either pull you down and thwart your efforts to reach your goals or help you create the life you want.

Remember these key thoughts from this week's study:
- Character is important in choosing your friends because their character will impact you.
- Your friends will either lift you up or pull you down.
- The best option is to seek out friends who will support you and help shape you into God's man.
- You will either contribute to the lives of your friends or take away from them.

PRAY TOGETHER

The Seriousness
of Support

goals for growth

☐ Realize that personal support is vital for men

☐ Identify the kinds of support each man needs

☐ Examine our willingness to be available to other men as a source of support

A men's small group is a great place for what we call the Four Cs: connection (mutuality), confession (authenticity), caring (ministry), and completion (maturity). We find that guys who meet frequently, who care about the spiritual welfare of their friends, and who can talk honestly about their struggles make steady progress personally, spiritually, and relationally. In a men's small group, secrets lose their power as God's people become God's presence and deliver God's provision for individuals in the group.

More specifically, God's plan is not for a man to turn to himself for answers when he is in crisis. Rather, he is called to turn to God and to His people for help and support. For men, turning to God alone seems fine, even preferred, because they can avoid the potential embarrassment that comes with vulnerability and confession. After all, we have our images to maintain and our egos to preserve.

Most men will, at great cost, choose isolation and endure frustration or unrelenting loneliness just to protect themselves. The great failing of this approach is that the longer a man remains unsupported and alone with his struggles, the worse he becomes.

On the other hand, men everywhere are discovering that they aren't alone in their struggles with their marriages, their finances, their spiritual growth, and their careers—other men share those same struggles. As King Solomon reflected, "There is nothing new under the sun" (Ecclesiastes 1:9).

KEY VERSES

A friend loves at all times, and a brother is born for a difficult time. (Proverbs 17:17)

15 This you know: All those in Asia have turned away from me, including Phygelus and Hermogenes. 16 May the Lord grant mercy to the household of Onesiphorus, because he often refreshed me and was not ashamed of my chains. 17 On the contrary, when he was in Rome, he diligently searched for me and found me. 18 May the Lord grant that he obtain mercy from Him on that day. And you know very well how much he ministered at Ephesus. (2 Timothy 1:15-18)

9 Make every effort to come to me soon, 10 for Demas has deserted me, because he loved this present world, and has gone to Thessalonica. Crescens has gone to Galatia, Titus to Dalmatia. 11 Only Luke is with me. Bring Mark with you, for he is useful to me in the ministry. 12 I have sent Tychicus to Ephesus. 13 When you come, bring the cloak I left in Troas with Carpus, as well as the scrolls, especially the parchments. (2 Timothy 4:9-13)

NOTES

_____

_____

_____

_____

_____

_____

_____

_____

_____

_____

_____

_____

_____

_____

_____

_____

_____

CONNECT WITH THE WORD

THIS SECTION IS DESIGNED TO BE A PERSONAL BIBLE STUDY
EXPERIENCE FOR YOU TO COMPLETE BEFORE YOUR SMALL-GROUP
SESSION EACH WEEK. COME TO YOUR GROUP MEETING PREPARED
TO SHARE YOUR RESPONSES AND PERSONAL APPLICATIONS. YOU
MAY WANT TO MARK OR HIGHLIGHT ANY QUESTIONS THAT WERE
PARTICULARLY MEANINGFUL TO YOU. BEFORE YOU BEGIN YOUR
STUDY, READ THE SCRIPTURES ON PAGE 44.

1. Read 2 Timothy 1:15-18 and 4:9-13 and consider what it looks
like for one man to support another. What, specifically, does it look
like in today's world?

2. What is being compared and contrasted in 1:15-18? What did
Phygelus and Hermogenes do when the chips were down?

3. How does the passage describe Onesiphorus (which means
"help bringer" in Greek)?

4. What was Paul's experience with Onesiphorus in the past? What do you think Paul's first thought was when he saw Onesiphorus from the confines of a prison?

5. Onesiphorus stepped into Paul's life when things were darkest. What does this tell you about the kind of man he was? Why is it often hard for men to step into another man's problems or needs?

6. How many men do you see in Paul's life in 4:9-13? What roles did they play?

REVIEW

What has the Lord revealed to you over the past week regarding the influence other men can have on your life?

The opening to this week's study says, "The longer a man remains unsupported and alone with his struggles, the worse he becomes." How have you seen this truth play out in your own life or in the life of someone close to you?

VIDEO TEACHING

▶ BELOW YOU WILL FIND A LISTENING GUIDE THAT GIVES
YOU AN OPPORTUNITY TO FOLLOW IMPORTANT POINTS
AS YOU VIEW THE MESSAGE FROM KENNY. WE'LL UNPACK THIS
INFORMATION TOGETHER AFTER THE VIDEO.

Watch Video Session 4: "The Seriousness of Support" (13:26).

When it comes to stresses and pressures in your life, don't make the assumption that you're _____.

It's one thing to hear where a man is feeling pressure and stress. It's another thing altogether to _____ _____ that pressure with him.

Support from true friendship:
    1. Relieves _____
    2. Reduces the _____
    3. Raises a man's _____
    4. Touches a man's _____

IF YOU MISSED THIS WEEK'S VIDEO VISIT
LIFEWAY.COM/FRIENDSHIP TO GET CAUGHT UP.

VIDEO FEEDBACK

■ In his video message, Kenny shares a list of benefits that come out of the support of true friendship. Which of those benefits most resonates with you and why?

Kenny also talks about our role in supporting other men. How well are you doing at lightening the load of other men in your life? What things are you doing/can you do to come alongside those who need your support?

CONNECT WITH THE GROUP

Jay's men's group meets every other Friday morning at a local coffeehouse and while it is hard to rally the troops at 6:30 AM, no one complains. They've been meeting for the last three years and are now accustomed to stepping into the hard spaces of one another's lives. They are so connected that no subject is taboo, especially if one of them is struggling with something. These men conduct spiritual business, study God's Word for advice they can trust, share their weaknesses with one another, pray for one another, and hold one another accountable to live as God's men.[1]

1. List some characteristics of Jay's group that are like and unlike your own men's group.

2. Based on 2 Timothy 1:15-18 and 4:9-13, what do God's men do for one another?

3. What does refreshing (breathing new life into, encouraging) a brother look like today in practical terms?

4. Why is it hard for men to receive help from other men? What is your experience with this?

Back to Jay's group. Recently Shaun reported that he hasn't visited Internet porn sites as he used to. Matt described the "good flow" that he and his wife have been enjoying, which was an answer to prayer after his previous week's doghouse tale. When Jeff announced that his sister was recently diagnosed with Hodgkin's disease, Travis felt led to offer Jeff a frequent flyer ticket to Denver to visit her. As for Jay, he took advantage of the time to confess that he is struggling to reconnect with his wife, Alene, and asked for advice on how to break through feelings of resentment that keep him from loving his wife the way God loves him. [2]

5. What is the spiritual impact on a man when he receives support from others? Relate a personal story about this, if possible.

6. In what area(s) of your life do you need the support of your brothers in Christ?

7. Who do you know that is going through a rough time these days? What can you do to support him and help him experience God's presence?

1. Adapted from Stephen Arterburn and Kenny Luck, Every Man, God's Man (Colorado Springs: WaterBrook Press, 2003), 145-6.
2. Ibid.

WRAP

Guys who meet frequently care about the spiritual welfare of their brothers and can honestly talk about the struggles and challenges they face. In a men's small group, secrets lose their power as God's Word is brought to bear on the issues at hand. Besides, it feels good to have someone watching your back. That's how God's man feels connected. [3]

Remember these key thoughts from this week's study:
- Personal support is vital for men.
- God's plan is for you to turn to Him and to His people for help and support.
- The longer you remain unsupported and alone with your struggles, the worse they become.
- A part of being God's man in your relationships is coming alongside other men who need your support.

PRAY TOGETHER

3. Adapted from Stephen Arterburn and Kenny Luck, *Every Man, God's Man* (Colorado Springs: WaterBrook Press, 2003), 145-6.

The Courage
to Confess

If you haven't figured this out by now, women spell intimacy T–A–L–K.

When emotions surface, women must verbally process them until no meat is left on the bone. Have you ever noticed that when a woman is feeling stressed out or angry, she will often call a friend to talk it over? Women are quick to express their feelings to others because they are hard-wired by God to be relational, nurturing, and emotionally connected. The bottom line is: These wonderfully complex creatures deal with their feelings.

We men, however, tend to run for the hills—all alone—when it comes to dealing with our emotions. We are not good at facing our feelings.

This is what we see playing out in men's lives: We hide and mask anger. We internalize pressure. We bury losses. We deny being wounded. We withdraw in the face of hard truth. We perceive openness as weakness. We push people away. We change the scenery. We keep secrets. We ignore the facts. We deceive ourselves. We close off. We fear failure. We deflect mistakes. We blame others. We excuse ourselves from feeling the hurts of others. We hide struggles. We change the subject.

But God says, "My power is made perfect in weakness" (2 Corinthians 12:9, NIV).

goals for growth

☐ Recognize the need to practice biblical openness and confession with other men

☐ Understand the consequences of living a secret life of sin

☐ Embrace the practice of being honest with God, with ourselves, and with others

KEY VERSES

The one who conceals his sins
will not prosper,
but whoever confesses and renounces them
will find mercy. *(Proverbs 28:13)*

[11] *Don't participate in the fruitless works of darkness, but instead expose them.* [12] *For it is shameful even to mention what is done by them in secret.* [13] *Everything exposed by the light is made clear,* [14] *for what makes everything clear is light. Therefore it is said:*
Get up, sleeper, and rise up from the dead,
and the Messiah will shine on you. (Ephesians 5:11-14)

Confess your sins to one another and pray for one another, so that you may be healed. (James 5:16)

NOTES

CONNECT WITH THE WORD

THIS SECTION IS DESIGNED TO BE A PERSONAL BIBLE STUDY EXPERIENCE FOR YOU TO COMPLETE BEFORE YOUR SMALL-GROUP SESSION EACH WEEK. COME TO YOUR GROUP MEETING PREPARED TO SHARE YOUR RESPONSES AND PERSONAL APPLICATIONS. YOU MAY WANT TO MARK OR HIGHLIGHT ANY QUESTIONS THAT WERE PARTICULARLY MEANINGFUL TO YOU. BEFORE YOU BEGIN YOUR STUDY, READ THE SCRIPTURES ON PAGE 56.

1. Read Proverbs 28:13. What is the downside of keeping secrets? Why is it not OK for us to pretend we have it all together?

2. What do we find on the other side of confession? How does this compare to what we often think will happen?

3. Read Ephesians 5:11-14 and James 5:16. We know we need to confess our sins to God, but why do you think God tells us to confess our sins to one another as well? (See also 1 John 1:9.)

4. According to Ephesians 5:11-14, what is the benefit of exposing our secrets? Be specific.

5. Based on these passages, what is the outcome of practicing biblical openness and confession? What do you think it looks like today in practical terms?

REVIEW

What has the Lord revealed to you over the past week regarding developing a support system of other God's men?

How would you define *confession* in your own words?

VIDEO TEACHING

BELOW YOU WILL FIND A LISTENING GUIDE THAT GIVES YOU AN OPPORTUNITY TO FOLLOW IMPORTANT POINTS AS YOU VIEW THE MESSAGE FROM KENNY. WE'LL UNPACK THIS INFORMATION TOGETHER AFTER THE VIDEO.

Watch Video Session 5: "The Courage to Confess" (12:16).

Being fully known takes _____.

Quoting your sins and struggles takes _____.

Sharing your pain takes _____.

Healthy masculinity = _____ and _____.

That's what the Bible calls _____.

How do you make sure there are no dark corners?

1. To be full of light, you need to bring your _____ into the light.

2. To be clean, you have to come _____.

3. To have His power, you have to present your _____.

IF YOU MISSED THIS WEEK'S VIDEO VISIT LIFEWAY.COM/FRIENDSHIP TO GET CAUGHT UP.

VIDEO FEEDBACK

 In his video message, Kenny shares that:
Being fully known takes *guts*.
Quoting your sins and struggles takes *faith*.
Sharing your pain takes *courage*.

Do those points help move you closer to or further away from confessing what's going on in your life to other godly men? Explain.

After watching the video message, how is your definition of *confession* changing?

CONNECT WITH THE GROUP

One time when I [Kenny] was in Sacramento, a guy confronted me about the issue of confession by asking point-blank: "So, Kenny, what's in it for me if I take the risk and confess?"

"Do you want more of God's power in your life?" I responded.
"Yes."
"Do you want to deal Satan a right-hand straight to the jaw?"
"Absolutely," he smiled.
"Do you want people to trust you and be close to you?"
"Sure."
"Do you want God to use you more?"
"With all my heart."
"Good. Then no secrets." [1]

1. What are the benefits and the drawbacks of confessing to other men? Why is confession hard for men today?

2. What are the practical benefits of being honest about where you really are or what you are struggling with?

3. How do think the Enemy views confession? Why?

4. What help does confession give to those who hear it in a safe group context?

The Scriptures encourage honest confession because it produces awesome results in the life of God's man. When God said, "My power is made perfect in weakness" (2 Corinthians 12:9, NIV), He was saying that when God's man is at his most vulnerable, that's when God's power flows most freely toward him. Confession puts us in that place. [2]

5. When have you experienced the benefits of confessing a struggle to another brother?

6. How can we help other men feel safe to share their most personal struggles?

7. Is there something from your past or something happening right now that needs to come out? Will you commit to sharing it with another man you trust? Why or why not?

1. Adapted from Stephen Arterburn and Kenny Luck, *Every Man, God's Man* (Colorado Springs: WaterBrook Press, 2003), 159-60.
2. Ibid.

WRAP

Most of us have been trained to treat our emotions like smelly socks that we stash in the back of a drawer, as far away as possible. When a man's emotions surface, the Sweeper (as we call him) comes in to methodically and logically neutralize the threat that a rogue emotion might present. He's that subconscious character in every man who works to eliminate emotions and makes logical arguments for acting the opposite way. His job is to keep any touchy situation from heating up too much, while sweeping stray emotions back under the rug where they belong.

God gave us emotions, just like He has emotions—we are made in His image. And avoiding our emotions is not at all how He intends for us to live.

Remember these key thoughts from this week's study:
- God intends for you to practice biblical openness and confession with other men.
- There are consequences for living a secret life of sin.
- When God's man is at his most vulnerable, that's when God's power flows most freely toward him.

PRAY TOGETHER

Empowered
to Encourage

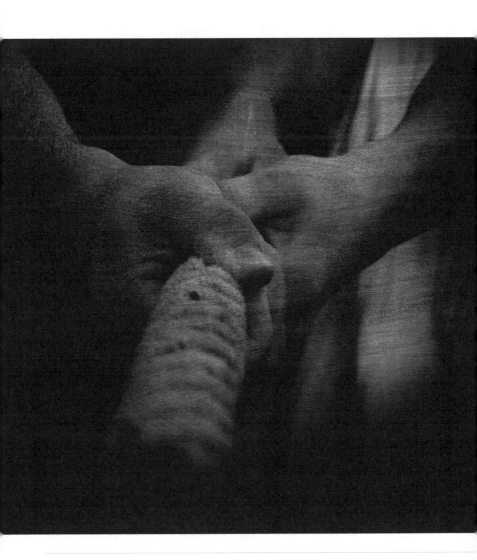

Several years ago my friends and I (Kenny) met at the local bagel shop for the purpose of reconnecting with one another as men. We needed to do this because, while we were accustomed to connecting socially (with or without our wives), we needed some "guy time" to discuss male issues. Even though we had been getting together off and on for years, this meeting was different—especially for me.

When the conversation paused and steered my way, I said, "When I come here, I don't have the luxury of walking away without doing real business spiritually. This is my one opportunity to get real with people I trust to help me." Let's just say I had everyone's attention.

"Can we cut the bull and get honest about at least one thing we know is bugging us—or one thing God is showing us about ourselves that we need to work on? I think guys—including me—are leaving here sometimes without advice or encouragement on the one thing they really need help with. Can we commit to that?"

Smart friends—the discerning ones—ask good questions, draw a man out, and see if they can encourage or affirm him in some way. It's like giving a guy a cup of cold water in the desert.

goals for growth

☐ Embrace the responsibility of being a source of encouragement to others

☐ Learn to allow other men to encourage us spiritually and personally

☐ Identify specific ways we can encourage others

KEY VERSES

The LORD will be a witness between you and me. (1 Samuel 20:42)

13 So David and his men, numbering about 600, left Keilah at once and moved from place to place. When it was reported to Saul that David had escaped from Keilah, he called off the expedition. 14 David then stayed in the wilderness strongholds and in the hill country of the Wilderness of Ziph. Saul searched for him every day, but God did not hand David over to him.
15 David was in the Wilderness of Ziph in Horesh when he saw that Saul had come out to take his life. 16 Then Saul's son Jonathan came to David in Horesh and encouraged him in his faith in God, 17 saying, "Don't be afraid, for my father Saul will never lay a hand on you. You yourself will be king over Israel, and I'll be your second-in-command. Even my father Saul knows it is true." 18 Then the two of them made a covenant in the Lord's presence. Afterward, David remained in Horesh, while Jonathan went home. (1 Samuel 23:13-18)

NOTES

_____

_____

_____

_____

_____

_____

_____

_____

_____

_____

_____

_____

_____

_____

_____

CONNECT WITH THE WORD

THIS SECTION IS DESIGNED TO BE A PERSONAL BIBLE STUDY
EXPERIENCE FOR YOU TO COMPLETE BEFORE YOUR SMALL-GROUP
SESSION EACH WEEK. COME TO YOUR GROUP MEETING PREPARED
TO SHARE YOUR RESPONSES AND PERSONAL APPLICATIONS. YOU
MAY WANT TO MARK OR HIGHLIGHT ANY QUESTIONS THAT WERE
PARTICULARLY MEANINGFUL TO YOU. BEFORE YOU BEGIN YOUR
STUDY, READ THE SCRIPTURES ON PAGE 68.

1. Read 1 Samuel 23:13-18. Describe David's circumstances before
Jonathan showed up.

2. What could Jonathan do for David that 600 other men could
not? Why did David need Jonathan more than his entire army?

3. What specific issues was David dealing with that Jonathan
addressed? What did Jonathan do for David that David couldn't
do for himself?

4. What did it cost Jonathan to do what he did for David? What did he risk?

5. Why do you think these two men sealed their relationship with a covenant (promise) before the Lord?

6. Why does adding this spiritual dimension to your friendships make them stronger?

REVIEW

What has the Lord revealed to you over the past week regarding practicing biblical openness and confession with other God's men?

How important is it to you to receive encouragement? How would you rate yourself on encouraging others? Explain.

VIDEO TEACHING

BELOW YOU WILL FIND A LISTENING GUIDE THAT GIVES YOU AN OPPORTUNITY TO FOLLOW IMPORTANT POINTS AS YOU VIEW THE MESSAGE FROM KENNY. WE'LL UNPACK THIS INFORMATION TOGETHER AFTER THE VIDEO.

Watch Video Session 6: "Empowered to Encourage" (13:23).

All men are starving for _____.

One of the most powerful _____ _____ is encouragement.

1. Believers need _____, _____ encouragement.

2. Believers who are under-encouraged get vulnerable to _____.

3. Believers have exclusive authority to encourage other _____.

IF YOU MISSED THIS WEEK'S VIDEO VISIT LIFEWAY.COM/FRIENDSHIP TO GET CAUGHT UP.

VIDEO FEEDBACK

In Kenny's video message he shares, "All men are hungry for encouragement." Why do you think that is so difficult for so many men to admit?

Consider how encouraging you are to the other men in your life. What steps can you take this week to move you closer to being the encourager they need you to be?

CONNECT WITH THE GROUP

A number of years ago, when I (Todd) lived in Chicago, I experienced a job crisis. It happened so fast, I was thoroughly caught off guard. It knocked the air out of me. Facing an uncertain future and living far away from home and the support of family and friends, I struggled to cope with my crisis alone.

My midweek call back home to my brother in California was a tough one. I didn't quite know what to say. Yet I guess I didn't need to say much. Dave and my brother-in-law, Bob, caught a red-eye flight into O'Hare that weekend and arrived Saturday morning.

1. When have you hit rock bottom in a career crisis or other kind of difficulty? Who helped pull you out of the depths?

2. Would you ever do something like Dave and Bob did? Why or why not?

The sacrificial act of encouragement by Dave and Bob was more than I could ever have hoped for. Here were two of my closest buddies, reaching out to me in a mega-act of kindness. And I was hurting more than I realized. The fact that they would spend the money and time away from their families to trek halfway across the country just to encourage me meant more than any phone call or card I received during my hardship.

3. What does spiritual encouragement look like among men? What things often prevent us from encouraging other men spiritually?

4. What man has personally encouraged you to do what God is calling you to do for Him? Explain.

5. In 1 Samuel 23:18, David and Jonathan made a solemn covenant before the Lord. What would that look like for us as a group?

6. What will it cost you personally to be a spiritual encourager to someone else?

7. How effective are you as a spiritual encourager? How can you tell?

Dave, Bob, and I ended up having a great weekend together. We rented cross-county skis and headed for a forest preserve. That night we took a train into the city for dinner. By Sunday I realized we hadn't even talked much about the career crisis I was facing. We didn't need to. I just needed to know someone cared about me and what I was going through. A show of love well worth its price!

8. Who do you know who needs encouragement to persevere in their faith? What can you do to encourage this person?

WRAP

Whether we want to admit it or not, we all need encouragement in our journey through life, especially during challenging times. And if we're honest with ourselves we'll realize that as much as we need encouragement from the other God's men in our lives, they need the same from us. It's a two-way street. It's what makes us complete in Christ. Because it is these relationships that bring about change in our character, convictions, conduct, and commitment to do life God's way.

Remember these key thoughts from this week's study:
- You have a responsibility to be a source of encouragement to other men.
- You need to allow other men to encourage you spiritually and personally.
- Whether they are willing to admit it or not, all men need to know someone cares about them and what they are going through.

PRAY TOGETHER

Getting Into Each Other's Spaces

No man I (Kenny) know joyfully embraces confrontation. Especially when it involves issues in his "personal airspaces" of life. Those are the areas we love to keep close to the chest, under our own personal control, and posted with large signs declaring, "NO TRESPASSING!"

Some of our razor-wired areas include our financial habits, our relationship with God, our relationship with our wife, our parenting approaches, and our moral views. These are sensitive areas because they involve personal values and core character issues.

But as we'll see in this week's study, the test of a true friend is his ability to engage in loving confrontation. In fact, you really don't have a true friendship unless you are willing to confront each other when it's needed. Confrontation requires courage and a strong relationship on both sides. And, most important, it requires trust in God and the man He is using—the man called your friend.

goals for growth

☐ Recognize that God encourages loving confrontation among brothers

☐ Commit to opening ourselves up to input from godly friends

☐ Seek to develop friendships with men who will tell us what we need to hear rather than only what we want to hear

KEY VERSES

Let the righteous one strike me—
it is an act of faithful love;
let him rebuke me—
it is oil for my head;
let me not refuse it.
Even now my prayer is against
the evil acts of the wicked.
(Psalm 141:5)

5 Better an open reprimand
than concealed love.
6 The wounds of a friend are trustworthy,
but the kisses of an enemy are excessive. (Proverbs 27:5-6)

19 My brothers, if any among you strays from the truth, and someone
turns him back, 20 let him know that whoever turns a sinner from the
error of his way will save his life from death and cover a multitude of
sins. (James 5:19-20)

NOTES

CONNECT WITH THE WORD

THIS SECTION IS DESIGNED TO BE A PERSONAL BIBLE STUDY
EXPERIENCE FOR YOU TO COMPLETE BEFORE YOUR SMALL-GROUP
SESSION EACH WEEK. COME TO YOUR GROUP MEETING PREPARED
TO SHARE YOUR RESPONSES AND PERSONAL APPLICATIONS. YOU
MAY WANT TO MARK OR HIGHLIGHT ANY QUESTIONS THAT WERE
PARTICULARLY MEANINGFUL TO YOU. BEFORE YOU BEGIN YOUR
STUDY, READ THE SCRIPTURES ON PAGE 80.

1. Read Proverbs 27:5-6 and James 5:19-20. What does an open
rebuke look like in a healthy relationship? How can a rebuke
demonstrate love?

2. How do you wound, but not kill, a friend?

3. To what extent do you need to trust your confronter in order
to be helped by him? What kind of friend is able, in your view,
to confront in love for good effect? What has to be there?

4. What's the difference between just being nice and expressing true care and concern for someone?

5. According to these passages, what kinds of friends do men really need?

6. What picture do you see in James? What does James say is the result of turning a man away from sin and back toward God?

REVIEW

What has the Lord revealed to you over the past week regarding encouraging other men as well as accepting encouragement for yourself?

When you think of someone speaking truth into your life, what does that look like to you?

VIDEO TEACHING

▶ BELOW YOU WILL FIND A LISTENING GUIDE THAT GIVES YOU AN OPPORTUNITY TO FOLLOW IMPORTANT POINTS AS YOU VIEW THE MESSAGE FROM KENNY. WE'LL UNPACK THIS INFORMATION TOGETHER AFTER THE VIDEO.

Watch Video Session 7: "Getting Into Each Other's Spaces" (10:37).

What is the consequence of not giving men in our lives freedom to ask questions?

We will plateau in our _____ or become blind in our _____.

As God's men, we are called to chuck our pride and submit to the authority and accountability of God's _____ and of God's _____.

We are deputized by Jesus to firmly, lovingly, and gently encourage a brother to line up his _____ and _____ to God with his _____.

IF YOU MISSED THIS WEEK'S VIDEO VISIT LIFEWAY.COM/FRIENDSHIP TO GET CAUGHT UP.

VIDEO FEEDBACK

In his video message, Kenny asks, "What is the consequence of not giving men in our lives freedom to ask questions?" What consequences have you seen play out in your own life or in the life of someone close to you?

How do you feel about submitting to "the authority and accountability of God's Word and of God's people"?

CONNECT WITH THE GROUP

I (Kenny) will never forget one night when two guys in the inner circle of my life stopped by to visit. What started out as a friendly meal turned into what felt like a fish fry … and the fish was me! Like skilled surgeons who knew exactly where to go and what to look for, they started making loving cuts in order to help me see the folly of masking over some serious issues arising between my wife and me. To put it mildly, when the conversation turned (on me), and the lights shined into the private corners of my life, it felt like a brutal stabbing rather than a benevolent surgery.

1. Why are we so uncomfortable with confrontation? What might help to change our perspective?

2. Why do you think both Solomon and James, the writers of Proverbs and the Book of James, present this issue as if there is no other option for God's man? What's at stake here?

When my friends confronted me, my defenses came up and out. But my friends have spines. They were strong and loving enough to break down my resistance and help me see the truth in their words. Was it uncomfortable? Definitely. Was it necessary? Absolutely. And it was all done out of deep love. For me.

3. According to James 5:19, when do you know that confronting is the right thing to do?

4. What steps can we take to begin practicing this kind of confrontation in our group? What will it require?

5. Are you personally open to healthy confrontation? Why or why not?

6. Do you know someone who needs to be lovingly confronted? Are you willing to get into his space and express your concern? Why or why not? What steps will you take to confront your friend?

Give someone—a man you respect spiritually and trust personally—the freedom to speak into your life if he sees or senses anything that might not be consistent with God's plan for you.

WRAP

The greatest temptation when we sense a confrontation needs to take place is not to do anything at all. But if we truly love the other man and care about his well-being, we have no choice. It's what God commanded and deep down it's what we want for our friend. Besides, don't we want the same for our own lives? Don't we pray that someone will love us enough to tell us the truth? How can we do less?

Remember these key thoughts from this week's study:
- God encourages loving confrontation among brothers.
- God wants you to develop friendships with men who will tell you what you need to hear rather than only what you want to hear.
- You really don't have a true friendship unless you are willing to confront each other when it's needed.

PRAY TOGETHER

Stretching One Another to Greatness for God

Years ago I (Kenny) left my job to launch Every Man Ministries. This was a new venture with a lot of unknowns. It was during this season of risk that Todd sent me the following letter:

Dear Kenny,

I often reflect back on the day you came by my office and told me you felt God leading you to help other men. Working with you on this the last four years has brought joy to my days. I have met few men with a passion to live with such tenacity as you. You have an uncontrollable drive to see men made new in Christ and walk free from sin and guilt. You desire to see men live out their manhood in the context of real life.

"All men die; few men really live." This could characterize your life. You have chosen a life that will not give you much of the world's goods. For that you will be blessed. As a result, you have become a model, a mentor, and a magnet for men. Attracted by your very life, they strive to be like the Christ who lives in you and through you.

Most men are nice. Few are dangerous. You are dangerous. You are willing to risk it all to see men complete in Christ.

Love you brother,
Todd

In our final session, we are going to look at the most significant way to help a friend: by stretching him to do something great for God.

goals for growth

☐ Understand God's true purpose for friendships among His men

☐ Recognize the need to help one another discover our personal ministry and mission on earth

☐ Commission one another to do the work God is calling us to do for Him

KEY VERSES

¹ Paul, an apostle of Christ Jesus by God's will, for the promise of life in Christ Jesus:

² To Timothy, my dearly loved son.

Grace, mercy, and peace from God the Father and Christ Jesus our Lord.

³ I thank God, whom I serve with a clear conscience as my ancestors did, when I constantly remember you in my prayers night and day.

⁴ Remembering your tears, I long to see you so that I may be filled with joy, ⁵ clearly recalling your sincere faith that first lived in your grandmother Lois, then in your mother Eunice, and that I am convinced is in you also.

⁶ Therefore, I remind you to keep ablaze the gift of God that is in you through the laying on of my hands. ⁷ For God has not given us a spirit of fearfulness, but one of power, love, and sound judgment.

⁸ So don't be ashamed of the testimony about our Lord, or of me His prisoner. Instead, share in suffering for the gospel, relying on the power of God. (2 Timothy 1:1-8)

Pleasant words are a honeycomb:
sweet to the taste and health to the body. (Proverbs 16:24)

Life and death are in the power of the tongue,
and those who love it will eat its fruit. (Proverbs 18:21)

A word spoken at the right time
is like gold apples on a silver tray. (Proverbs 25:11)

NOTES

CONNECT WITH THE WORD

THIS SECTION IS DESIGNED TO BE A PERSONAL BIBLE STUDY
EXPERIENCE FOR YOU TO COMPLETE BEFORE YOUR SMALL-GROUP
SESSION EACH WEEK. COME TO YOUR GROUP MEETING PREPARED
TO SHARE YOUR RESPONSES AND PERSONAL APPLICATIONS. YOU
MAY WANT TO MARK OR HIGHLIGHT ANY QUESTIONS THAT WERE
PARTICULARLY MEANINGFUL TO YOU. BEFORE YOU BEGIN YOUR
STUDY, READ THE SCRIPTURES ON PAGE 92.

1. Read 2 Timothy 1:1-8. Who's missing from Timothy's family in
this passage (v. 5)? What role did Paul play in Timothy's life?

2. What credibility does verse 3 give Paul to say what he says later
on in the passage? What message does this send to Timothy?

3. What do you think it means to "keep ablaze" the gift of God
within us (v. 6)?

4. What gifts has God already given every man in addition to his talents (v. 7)?

5. How was Paul stretching Timothy (v. 8)? Where was Paul taking Timothy in his faith?

6. Read Proverbs 16:24; 18:21; and 25:11. What do these passages say about the importance of the words we speak into another man's life?

7. How do encouraging and affirming words stretch men to greatness?

REVIEW

What has the Lord revealed to you over the past week regarding confrontation—being willing to confront in love as well as accept confrontation in love?

Share an experience when someone spoke a few well-chosen words to you that made a real difference in your life.

VIDEO TEACHING

BELOW YOU WILL FIND A LISTENING GUIDE THAT GIVES YOU AN OPPORTUNITY TO FOLLOW IMPORTANT POINTS AS YOU VIEW THE MESSAGE FROM KENNY. WE'LL UNPACK THIS INFORMATION TOGETHER AFTER THE VIDEO.

Watch Video Session 8: "Stretching One Another to Greatness for God" (14:53).

A red-zone friendship:
1. increases spiritual _____;
2. stimulates greater _____ to God's plan;
3. helps you _____ _____ other men in order to reach your goals as God's man.

1. God has an assignment for each man to _____ on earth.
2. That assignment is going to require _____ as well as _____ gifts.
3. The assignment is going to stretch each man's _____ and make him _____ God.

The job of God's man in the lives of his friends is to help them not miss the _____ that God has for them.

IF YOU MISSED THIS WEEK'S VIDEO VISIT LIFEWAY.COM/FRIENDSHIP TO GET CAUGHT UP.

VIDEO FEEDBACK

 Kenny talks about his "red-zone" friendships. On a scale of 1-10, how present is that level of friendship in your life?

1	10
I don't have any men in my life whom I trust on that level.	I have a group of men who help me accomplish my goals and allow me to do the same for them.

Share with your group what steps you will take after this study is complete to do life with a group of men who will make sure you don't miss your personal ministry and mission.

CONNECT WITH THE GROUP

Needing courage or to be encouraged is a common experience we all face as finite human beings, and we should never think it odd if we reach a place where we need to be encouraged. In fact, we often find the people of God in circumstances where they needed to be encouraged: "In fact, when we came into Macedonia, we had no rest. Instead, we were troubled in every way: conflicts on the outside, fears inside. But God, who comforts the humble, comforted us by the arrival of Titus, and not only by his arrival, but also by the comfort he received from you. He told us about your deep longing, your sorrow, and your zeal for me, so that I rejoiced even more" (2 Corinthians 7:5-7).

1. In what practical ways can we push one another to greater service in advancing God's kingdom?

2. How do we help one another overcome our fear of stepping out and serving God?

Do you think Todd's letter encouraged me and stretched me to keep pushing myself spiritually? Absolutely. King Solomon said it this way: "A word spoken at the right time is like gold apples on a silver tray" (Proverbs 25:11). Sometimes we don't realize a few well-chosen words can make a good man great.

3. According to 2 Timothy 1:7 and Proverbs 18:21, what is the key that empowers God's man to successfully fulfill his purpose on earth and use his gifts? What's our job? What's God's job?

4. What does it mean to be bold in our faith? What, if anything, is holding you back from encouraging another man to be bold in his faith? How can you verbally affirm another man's faith as Paul affirmed Timothy's?

5. Pick one guy in the group and affirm what you see God doing in his life. In what specific areas would you encourage him to step out more in his service to God? What steps would you encourage him to take to facilitate God's work in his life?

6. Based upon what you've learned in this study, what can you do and say in the coming months to affirm God's work in the lives of other men? To challenge others to use their gifts to the fullest? To encourage others toward a deeper and bolder expression of their faith?

Pray for one another, asking God to strengthen each man's faith and service to Him.

WRAP

Encouragement is finding (or helping others find) the courage, by God's grace and strength, to run the race He has laid out before us, no matter how difficult or painful the course. Encouragers simply encourage us to think, say, and do the things that are right and good. They know that if we are guided to see our strengths and are affirmed in who we are made to be, we will feel better and our world will also change for the better. We will experience more joy in our lives and less pain. And then at some point we will turn and give to others what has been given to us.

Remember these key thoughts from this week's study:
- God's true purpose for friendships among His men is to help one another discover their personal ministry and mission on earth.
- The most significant way to help a friend is by stretching him to do something great for God.
- Encouragement comes from having someone in your life who helps you find the courage to run the race God has laid out before you.

PRAY TOGETHER

Group Covenant

As you begin this study, it is important that your group covenant together, agreeing to live out important group values. Once these values are agreed upon, your group will be on its way to experiencing true Christian community. It's very important that your group discuss these values—preferably as you begin this study.

PRIORITY: While in this group, we will give the group meetings priority.

PARTICIPATION: Everyone is encouraged to participate and no one dominates.

RESPECT: Everyone is given the right to his own opinions, and all questions are encouraged and respected.

CONFIDENTIALITY: Anything that is said in our meetings is never repeated outside the meeting without permission.

LIFE CHANGE: We will regularly assess our progress toward applying the "steps" to an amazing life of passionately following Christ.

CARE AND SUPPORT: Permission is given to call upon each other at any time, especially in times of crisis. The group will provide care for every member.

ACCOUNTABILITY: We agree to let the members of our group hold us accountable to commitments we make in whatever loving ways we decide upon. Unsolicited advice giving is not permitted.

EMPTY CHAIR: Our group will work together to fill the empty chair with an unchurched man.

MISSION: We agree as a group to reach out and invite others to join us and to work toward multiplication of our group to form new groups.

MINISTRY: We will encourage one another to volunteer to serve in a ministry and to support missions work by giving financially and/or personally serving.

I, _____, agree to all of the above.

Date: _____

Leader Guide

We hope the information provided on the following pages will better equip you to lead your study of *Friendship: Transform Through Strong Relationships*. In addition to the general notes to help you along the way, we've included the answers for the video listening guides for each session. These may be useful to you if someone misses a session and would like to fill in the blanks.

This study is designed to cover an eight-week time frame. However, it is not unusual for a group to spend two or three meetings completing one session. Go for depth over distance. And don't hesitate to adapt this study so that it truly works for you.

Note: You may consider bringing your men together before your first official meeting to pass out member books or just to give them an opportunity to check things out before they commit to the study. This would be a great time to show the Get Healthy Series overview (10:03) to those in attendance so they can get an introduction to the series. You will find this overview on the DVD in your Leader Kit.

SESSION 01_THE MYTH OF ISOLATION

Key Verses and Goals for Growth—You'll want to review these items as you prepare for each small-group session.

Introduction—Each session begins with a narrative overview of the weekly topic. This material is designed to help you introduce the topic of study. You will want to read this before your group meets so that you'll better understand the topic and the context for your time together. For weeks 2-8, suggest that group members read this before you meet.

Personal Time: Connect with the Word—Each member of your small group should complete this section *before* the small-group meeting. In order for them to have the opportunity to complete this portion of the study before your first meeting, ask group members to purchase their workbooks in advance or make plans to get workbooks to them ahead of time.

Group Time: Review—In weeks 2-8 the first question in this section will be used to talk about what God has been revealing to group members from their time with Him during the week. In this first session, however, you'll talk in more broad terms about your expectations and the dangers of living your lives like spiritual castaways. These questions are intended to be nonthreatening to group members so that a pattern of participation can be established early on.

Group Time: Video Teaching—Encourage group members to follow along, fill in the blanks on page 13, and take additional notes as they hear things that speak strongly to their own stories.

> The single greatest attack that men have to fear is isolation—being <u>emotionally</u>, <u>relationally</u>, and <u>spiritually</u> cut off from other men.

> God's man is never instructed to self-diagnose his own <u>character</u>.

> You need friends, not <u>fans</u>.

Group Time: Video Feedback—This section is designed as follow-up to the video message. You will want to use the listening guide to highlight the main teaching points from the video and process with the group what they heard and how they were affected.

Group Time: Connect with the Group—In Session 01 you will talk as a group about the dangers of isolation and how pursuing healthy friendships is a way of life that provides help when they need it most.

Wrap—At this point each week, you will close the group time in prayer. You may want to use this time to reflect on and respond to what God has done in your group during the session. Invite group members to share their personal joys and concerns. For this week, it's probably best for you to pray for the group. In coming weeks, as group members get more comfortable, consider asking for volunteers to lead the group in prayer.

SESSION 02_THE COMMAND TO CONNECT

Introduction—Welcome group members back. Use the narrative overview on page 19 to introduce the topic for Session 02. Make sure you read this before your group meets so that you'll better understand the topic and the context for your time together.

Personal Time: Connect with the Word—Encourage the men to use this as their personal Bible study for the week.

Group Time: Review—This week you will talk about what the Lord has revealed to you over the past week regarding coming out of isolation. In preparation for this week's topic, you'll talk about your primary purpose for friendship and how that lines up with the purpose described in Hebrews. Continue to encourage group members to share during this time.

Group Time: Video Teaching—Encourage group members to follow along, fill in the blanks on page 25, and take additional notes as they hear things that speak strongly to their own stories.

> God says that connecting with other men for the purpose of spiritual growth and accountability is not an <u>option</u>.
>
> Run <u>away</u> from temptation.
> Run <u>toward</u> God's purposes.
> Run <u>with</u> a group of men who are running after God's purposes.
>
> When you're <u>disconnected</u> not only do you suffer, but your other relationships suffer.
>
> When you <u>connect</u> and become more healthy, the other relationships in your life become more healthy.

Group Time: Connect with the Group—In Session 02 you will talk about how connecting with other men is important to their spiritual growth.

Wrap—This week consider asking a volunteer to pray. Ask the Lord to give you the courage you need to connect to other God's men.

SESSION 03_CONNECTING TO CHARACTER

Introduction—Use the narrative overview on page 31 to introduce the topic of study for Session 03. Read this before your group meets so that you'll better understand the topic and the context.

Personal Time: Connect with the Word—Encourage the men to use this as their personal Bible study for the week.

Group Time: Review—This week you will be talking about what the Lord has revealed to you over the past week regarding making consistent connection with God's men a part of your lives. In preparation for this week's topic you'll talk about which clique you identified with in school and how that group has influenced the person you are today.

Group Time: Video Teaching—Encourage group members to follow along, fill in the blanks on page 37, and take additional notes as they hear things that speak strongly to their own stories.

> Godly character is synonymous with <u>connecting</u> <u>consistently</u> with godly men.

> God's man must <u>search</u> <u>out</u> other godly men.

> Through the ages, God's men who have respected God's Word have sought God's men so that they could <u>accomplish</u> <u>God's</u> <u>will</u> in their lives.

Group Time: Connect with the Group—In Session 03 you will talk about the importance of character in choosing your friends.

Wrap—Close your group time in prayer, asking God for wisdom in choosing friends who will lift you up and not pull you down.

SESSION 04_THE SERIOUSNESS OF SUPPORT

Introduction—Use the narrative overview on page 43 to help you introduce the topic of study for Session 04.

Group Time: Review—This week you will be talking about what the Lord has revealed to you over the past week regarding the influence other men can have on your lives. In preparation for this week's topic, you'll talk about how your struggles will only get more difficult the longer you remain isolated and alone.

Group Time: Video Teaching—Encourage group members to follow along, fill in the blanks on page 49, and take additional notes as they hear things that speak strongly to their own stories.

When it comes to stresses and pressures in your life, don't make the assumption that you're <u>alone</u>.

It's one thing to hear where a man is feeling pressure and stress. It's another thing altogether to <u>step</u> <u>into</u> that pressure with him.

Support from true friendship:
1. Relieves <u>pressure</u>
2. Reduces the <u>load</u>
3. Raises a man's <u>spirit</u>
4. Touches a man's <u>soul</u>

Group Time: Connect with the Group—In Session 04 you will talk about God's plan for you to turn to Him and to His people for help and support.

Wrap—Request that a volunteer close your group time in prayer, asking God to help you faithfully follow God's plan and open up to the help and support of His people.

SESSION 05_THE COURAGE TO CONFESS

Introduction—Use the narrative overview on page 55 to help you introduce the topic of study for Session 05.

Group Time: Review—This week you will be talking about what the Lord has revealed to you over the past week regarding developing a support system of other God's men. In preparation for this week's topic, you'll talk about how you define the word *confession*.

Group Time: Video Teaching—Encourage group members to follow along, fill in the blanks on page 61, and take additional notes as they hear things that speak strongly to their own stories.

> Being fully known takes <u>guts</u>.
> Quoting your sins and struggles takes <u>faith</u>.
> Sharing your pain takes <u>courage</u>.
>
> Healthy masculinity = <u>transparency</u> and <u>authenticity</u>.
>   That's what the Bible calls <u>confession</u>.
>
> How do you make sure there are no dark corners?
>   1. To be full of light, you need to bring your <u>darkness</u> into the light.
>   2. To be clean, you have to come <u>clean</u>.
>   3. To have His power, you have to present your <u>problems</u>.

Group Time: Connect with the Group—In Session 05 you will learn about biblical openness and confession with other men.

Wrap—Request that a volunteer close your group time in prayer, asking God to help you be courageous enough to expose your dark corners to the light.

SESSION 06_EMPOWERED TO ENCOURAGE

Introduction—Use the narrative overview on page 67 to help you introduce the topic of study for Session 06.

Group Time: Review—This week you will be talking about what the Lord has revealed to you over the past week regarding practicing biblical openness and confession with other God's men. In preparation for this week's topic, you'll talk about how important encouragement is to you.

Group Time: Video Teaching—Encourage group members to follow along, fill in the blanks on page 73, and take additional notes as they hear things that speak strongly to their own stories.

> All men are starving for <u>encouragement</u>.
>
> One of the most powerful <u>spiritual weapons</u> is encouragement.
>
> 1. Believers need <u>in-person, verbal</u> encouragement.
> 2. Believers who are under-encouraged get vulnerable to <u>evil</u>.
> 3. Believers have exclusive authority to encourage other <u>believers</u>.

Group Time: Connect with the Group—In Session 06 you will talk about your responsibility to offer encouragement as well as your need to accept encouragement.

Wrap—Close the group in prayer, thanking God for the gift of encouragement.

SESSION 07_GETTING INTO EACH OTHER'S SPACES

Introduction—Use the narrative overview on page 79 to help you introduce the topic of study for Session 07.

Group Time: Review—This week you will be talking about what the Lord has revealed to you over the past week regarding encouraging other men as well as accepting encouragement for yourselves. In preparation for this week's topic, you'll talk about what it looks like to you to have someone "speak truth into your life."

Group Time: Video Teaching—Encourage group members to follow along, fill in the blanks on page 85, and take additional notes as they hear things that speak strongly to their own stories.

What is the consequence of not giving men in our lives freedom to ask questions?

> We will plateau in our <u>growth</u> or become blind in our <u>pride</u>.

As God's men, we are called to chuck our pride and submit to the authority and accountability of God's <u>Word</u> and of God's <u>people</u>.

We are deputized by Jesus to firmly, lovingly, and gently encourage a brother to line up his <u>identity</u> and <u>responsibility</u> to God with his <u>activity</u>.

Group Time: Connect with the Group—In Session 07 you will talk about developing friendships with men who will tell you what you need to hear rather than only what you want to hear.

Wrap—Close the group in prayer, asking God to help you be willing to give other God's men freedom to speak truthfully into your life as well as courage to speak truth into the lives of others.

SESSION 08_STRETCHING ONE ANOTHER TO GREATNESS FOR GOD

Introduction—Use the narrative overview on page 91 to help you introduce the topic of study for Session 08.

Group Time: Review—This week you will be talking about what the Lord has revealed to you over the past week regarding being willing to confront in love as well as accept confrontation in love. In preparation for this week's topic, you'll talk about the difference it made in your life when someone spoke a few well-chosen words to you.

Group Time: Video Teaching—Encourage group members to follow along, fill in the blanks on page 97, and take additional notes as they hear things that speak strongly to their own stories.

A red-zone friendship:
1. increases spiritual <u>accountability</u>;
2. stimulates greater <u>obedience</u> to God's plan;
3. helps you <u>intentionally</u> <u>pursue</u> other men in order to reach your goals as God's man.

1. God has an assignment for each man to <u>fulfill</u> on earth.
2. That assignment is going to require <u>spiritual</u> as well as <u>natural</u> gifts.
3. The assignment is going to stretch each man's <u>faith</u> and make him <u>trust</u> God.

The job of God's man in the lives of his friends is to help them not miss the <u>mission</u> that God has for them.

Group Time: Connect with the Group—In Session 08 you will talk about God's true purpose for friendships among His men—to help one another discover your personal ministry and mission on earth. Also, be sure to discuss next steps with your group and encourage the men to Get In, Get Healthy, Get Strong, and Get Going. Go to LifeWay.com/Men for more help in developing your church's strategy for men.

Wrap—Ask as many group members as will to pray aloud, thanking God for this eight-week journey you have completed together.

Group Directory

Name: _____
Home Phone: _____
Mobile Phone: _____
E-mail: _____
Social Network(s): _____

Name: _____
Home Phone: _____
Mobile Phone: _____
E-mail: _____
Social Network(s): _____

Name: _____
Home Phone: _____
Mobile Phone: _____
E-mail: _____
Social Network(s): _____

Name: _____
Home Phone: _____
Mobile Phone: _____
E-mail: _____
Social Network(s): _____

Name: _____
Home Phone: _____
Mobile Phone: _____
E-mail: _____
Social Networks(s): _____

Name: _____
Home Phone: _____
Mobile Phone: _____
E-mail: _____
Social Network(s): _____

Name: _____
Home Phone: _____
Mobile Phone: _____
E-mail: _____
Social Network(s): _____

Name: _____
Home Phone: _____
Mobile Phone: _____
E-mail: _____
Social Network(s): _____

Name: _____
Home Phone: _____
Mobile Phone: _____
E-mail: _____
Social Network(s): _____

Name: _____
Home Phone: _____
Mobile Phone: _____
E-mail: _____
Social Network(s): _____

Name: _____
Home Phone: _____
Mobile Phone: _____
E-mail: _____
Social Network(s): _____

Name: _____
Home Phone: _____
Mobile Phone: _____
E-mail: _____
Social Network(s): _____

Name: _____
Home Phone: _____
Mobile Phone: _____
E-mail: _____
Social Network(s): _____

Name: _____
Home Phone: _____
Mobile Phone: _____
E-mail: _____
Social Network(s): _____